Science Technology Engineering Maths

STEM STARTERS FOR KIDS

BIOLOGY
ACTIVITY Book

Written by Jenny Jacoby

Science education consultant: Dr Sue Dale Tunnicliffe

Designed and illustrated by
Vicky Barker

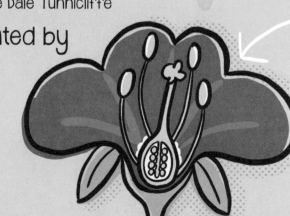

www.bsmall.co.uk

Published by
b small publishing ltd.

www.bsmall.co.uk

· 1 2 3 4 5 ·

Production by Madeleine Ehm
Design and art direction by Vicky Barker
Science education consultant: Dr Sue Dale Tunnicliffe
Printed in China by WKT Co. Ltd.

British Library
Cataloguing-in-
Publication Data.

A catalogue record for this
book is available from the
British Library.

ISBN
978-1-912909-13-1

WHAT IS BIOLOGY?

Biology is the area of science that studies life, living things and their environment. The study of biology can range from the tiniest bacteria up to the largest mammal, and from how your food is digested inside your body, to how a disease travels through a large group of people.

WHAT IS STEM?

STEM stands for 'science, technology, engineering and mathematics'. These four areas are closely linked, and biology is an important part of science. We need to understand how living things work, including humans, so that we can prevent harm and improve lives. The better we understand ourselves and other living organisms, the better we can look after them and protect the balance of life on our planet.

Science

Technology

Engineering

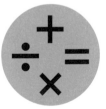
Maths

DIFFERENT PLANTS FOR DIFFERENT PLACES

A **habitat** is the natural environment for a plant or animal. A particular plant is **adapted** to live in a particular habitat, meaning they have changed over time to survive in that place. There are different groups of plants, such as flowering or ferns, with many types in each group.

Plants that live in the desert, where it is hot and there is very little rain, are adapted to not need much water and to thrive in the heat.

Thick, fleshy leaves — to store water

Waxy coating on the leaves — to keep water inside

Roots that travel a long way but not deep down — to absorb as much rain as quickly as possible when it does fall

Sharp spikes — to protect against animals searching for water

Plants that live where there are four different seasons are adapted to change through the year.

In summer, plenty of leaves to capture the sunlight to make food

In autumn, leaves change colour to make best use of the lower light

In winter, with less light and fiercer weather, tree conserves energy by losing all its leaves

Roots extend a long way to let the tree grow large and strong

Thick bark to stop water evaporating

4

oak tree

succulent

buttress roots

monstera

lime tree in autumn

cactus

Read about all three habitats before matching these plants to their environment. Draw a sun, raindrop or leaf next to each plant. Answers on page 30.

 desert rainforest deciduous forest

Plants that live in rainforests are adapted to deal with lots of rainfall.

Thin tree bark to help water to evaporate

Leaves have a pointy tip to help rain run off as quickly as possible

Thick buttresses to steady the tree because roots do not grow deeply in shallow soil

5

FROM SEEDS TO ADULTS

Most flowering plants grow from seeds. Although plants look different when they are fully grown, the way they start to grow is usually the same. A seed is dormant (like being asleep) until it is planted and has everything it needs to grow.

4. Root travels down

The root travels deeper into the soil in search of more water. It sends out side branches, which help to keep the seedling secure in the soil.

5. Shoot travels up

The shoot grows upwards in search of light. The seed has sprouted.

6. Leaf growing

The shoot grows leaves to help make food for the plant.

3. Root and shoot growing

Then a tiny root starts growing followed by a shoot.

1. Planting the seed

A seed needs to be planted in soil where it has enough water and the temperature is warm enough.

2. Starting to swell

Then it takes in water and starts to swell. This is called germination.

These seeds have started to grow. This is called germination.

Draw around the group of seeds that matches the one on the right. Answers on page 30.

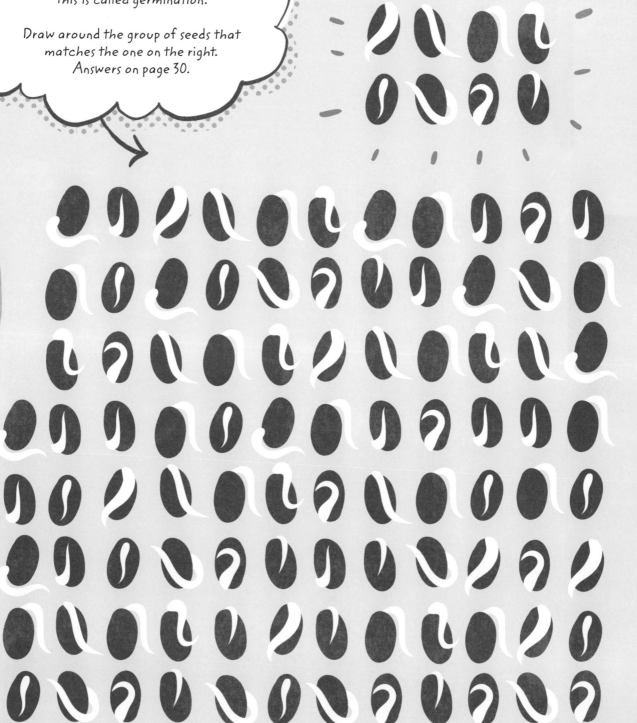

HOW FLOWERING PLANTS GROW

Plants need five key things to grow: sunlight, water, air, the right temperature and time.

temperature has to be warm enough but not too hot

leaves use the energy from **sunlight** to make food

leaves use carbon dioxide from the **air** to make food

Growing takes time!

roots absorb **water** with essential chemicals needed for growth from the soil

If any of the five things are missing, a plant cannot grow properly. Draw in the missing ingredients to help these plants to grow.

Anwers on page 30.

sunlight   temperature

time   air   water

THE LIFE CYCLE OF A FLOWER

Like all living things, plants start small and grow until they are able to produce new plants. It is a bit like having children. All plants eventually die, but their 'children' grow to make new plants. This is called a life cycle because it happens over and over again. Flowers are an important part of a plant's life cycle as they help to make new seeds.

1. Pollination

Powdery **pollen** is made inside the flower on the **anther** of the **stamens**. **Pollination** happens when pollen sticks on the **stigma** and travels down into the **ovule** to make seeds grow.

When insects or other animals visit flowers to gather nectar, pollen gets knocked off the stamens and lands on the insects or animals, which they carry to the other flowers they visit.

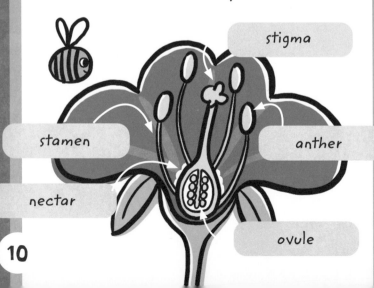

stigma

stamen

anther

nectar

ovule

2. Seeds

When the seeds have grown, they need to scatter to find their own place to grow into a new plant. Different plants have different ways of travelling.

by air

by animal

by bird
(this bird ate a blackberry and the seeds are scattered in its poo)

by water

ANIMAL ADAPTATION

Animals are adapted to the environment they live in. This adaptation happens over hundreds of thousands of years. The better suited a particular living thing is to its environment, the more likely it is to pass on its useful characteristics by having healthy children. Individuals who struggle to survive in an environment are less likely to have many healthy children so their less useful characteristics are not passed on.

Compare the African elephant with its extinct cousin, the woolly mammoth. They look very similar, but the elephant is adapted to live in the hot climates of Africa, while the woolly mammoth has adaptations to live in Europe during the last Ice Age.

wrinkly skin to help keep cool

large ears to help keep cool

small ears to stop heat loss

covered in thick fur to keep warm

These animals are adapted to a mixture of different environments. To help sort them, put a blue snowflake next to the animals that live in the cold and a red sun next to those that prefer hot environments. Ring a part of the animal that shows its adaptation.
Answers on page 31.

reindeer

polar bear

fennec fox

camel

walrus

scorpion

CLASSIFICATION

There are so many living things in the world – from bacteria too small to see, to the huge blue whale and giant redwood trees – that to make sense of how everything is related, we use classification. Each different type of living thing is called a species and all species are related to each other, even if very distantly.

By comparing the biology of different species we can begin to classify them into groups of similar species.

A mouse and a giraffe do not look very similar at first glance but they do actually have a lot in common. They are both in the group called **mammals.**

We have to be careful not to classify things just because they look similar. Birds and butterflies both fly with wings but they are not closely related. Birds are **vertebrate animals** (they have a back bone) and butterflies are **invertebrate** (no backbone) **insects.**

two eyes

feed milk to their children

fur

four limbs

feathers, two legs

six legs

wings, lay eggs

How many insects can you spot in
this picture? How many mammals?
Remember: insects have six legs.
Mammals have two or four.
Answers on page 31.

WHAT'S FOR DINNER?

Animals that only eat meat are called **carnivores**. And animals that only eat plants are called **herbivores**. Some animals eat everything and anything! They are called **omnivores**.

Not all carnivores hunt for the meat they eat. Some, such as hyenas and vultures, are called **scavengers**. They wait for other animals to do the hunting and eat what is left. Some carnivores are invertebrates, such as blowfly maggots, but unlike vertebrates they do not have teeth.

The shape of an animal's teeth can give clues about what it likes to eat.

CARNIVORES
Sharp teeth for tearing into meat

OMNIVORES
A combination of sharp teeth and flat molars

HERBIVORES
Wide and flat molars for grinding tough plants

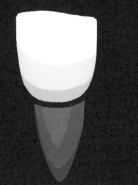

INCISOR

CANINE

PREMOLAR

MOLAR

Humans have incisor teeth, canines and molars.
What type of diet do humans have?

Menu

MEAT	VEGETARIAN	ANYTHING GOES!

Draw up a menu for the Animal Restaurant. Make sure there is something for everyone!

MAKING MORE

For an animal or plant to continue its life cycle it needs to produce young. Without making more individuals, the species would die out! In most animals, making young needs a male and a female. When a male and a female mate, and an egg is fertilised, a new 'baby' can grow.

For insects, fish, birds and reptiles, the female lays the fertilised egg, and eventually the baby hatches out. Mammals do not lay eggs but grow the baby inside the female until it is big enough to be born and survive in the world.

Different animals have very different life cycles but almost all animals need a male and a female to start the process.

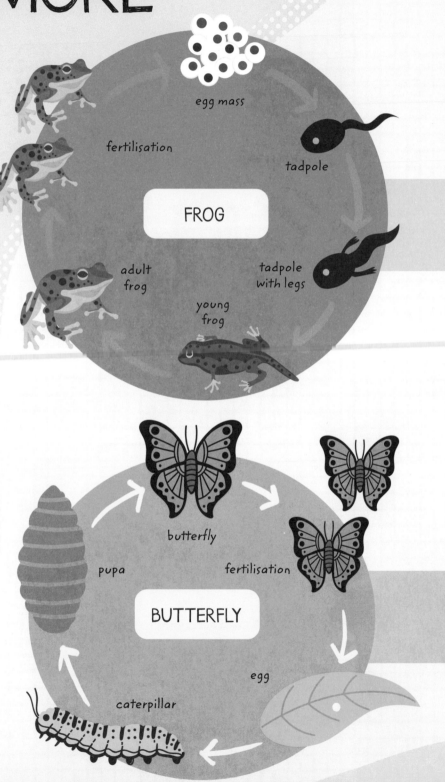

egg mass

tadpole

fertilisation

FROG

tadpole with legs

adult frog

young frog

butterfly

pupa

fertilisation

BUTTERFLY

egg

caterpillar

The life cycle of many animals happens over the course of a year, with young being born in the warmer spring months. Spot the frog, butterfly, chicken, rabbit and blackbird at different stages of their life cycles in the spring and the autumn pictures.
Answers on page 31.

HUMAN DIGESTION

It can take between one and two days for the food you eat to pass through your body and emerge as a poo! On its way, food goes on a long journey through what is called the **alimentary canal**. Food travels around 9 metres along the alimentary canal, from your mouth to your bottom.

The job of the alimentary canal is to take the nutrients from your food that your body needs. Anything the body does not need leaves your body as waste (a poo!). This process is called **digestion.**

1. Crunch! Your mouth breaks food down by chewing and mixing with saliva (spit). **Draw a chunk of apple in the mouth.**

2. It takes about 3 seconds to swallow.

Complete the drawing to help the food travel through the alimentary canal!

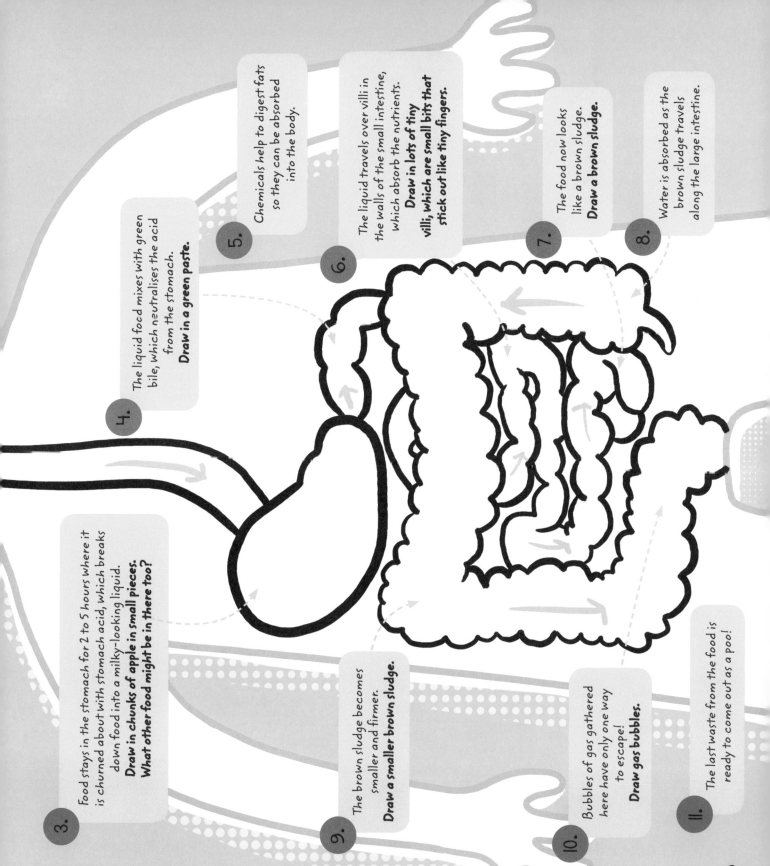

3. Food stays in the stomach for 2 to 5 hours where it is churned about with stomach acid, which breaks down food into a milky-looking liquid. **Draw in chunks of apple in small pieces. What other food might be in there too?**

4. The liquid food mixes with green bile, which neutralises the acid from the stomach. **Draw in a green paste.**

5. Chemicals help to digest fats so they can be absorbed into the body.

6. The liquid travels over villi in the walls of the small intestine, which absorb the nutrients. **Draw in lots of tiny villi, which are small bits that stick out like tiny fingers.**

7. The food now looks like a brown sludge. **Draw a brown sludge.**

8. Water is absorbed as the brown sludge travels along the large intestine.

9. The brown sludge becomes smaller and firmer. **Draw a smaller brown sludge.**

10. Bubbles of gas gathered here have only one way to escape! **Draw gas bubbles.**

11. The last waste from the food is ready to come out as a poo!

21

SKELETONS

A skeleton is the frame for the body and all vertebrate animals have bones in the same basic pattern. Invertebrates have a different kind of skeleton. Bones give strength and a structure for muscles and organs to build around, and help everything stay in the right place. They also protect the soft parts inside the body. As our body grows, so does our skeleton.

DID YOU KNOW?

There are 206 bones in the human body but babies are born with 270! That's because there are some bones that are a single piece in an adult, such as the skull, that start off as several smaller pieces. Those pieces can move about a little, so the skull can squash together. This makes it easier for a baby to be born, and gives the baby's brain space to grow. The skull bones fuse together into one bone by the age of two.

Bony quiz!
Look at the skeleton to answer these questions.
Answers on page 32.

1. How many bones make up a single finger?

2. Which is the strongest bone?

3. Which is the longest bone?

4. Which is the smallest bone?

5. How many pairs of ribs are there?

6. What is the jawbone called?

7. What is the kneecap called?

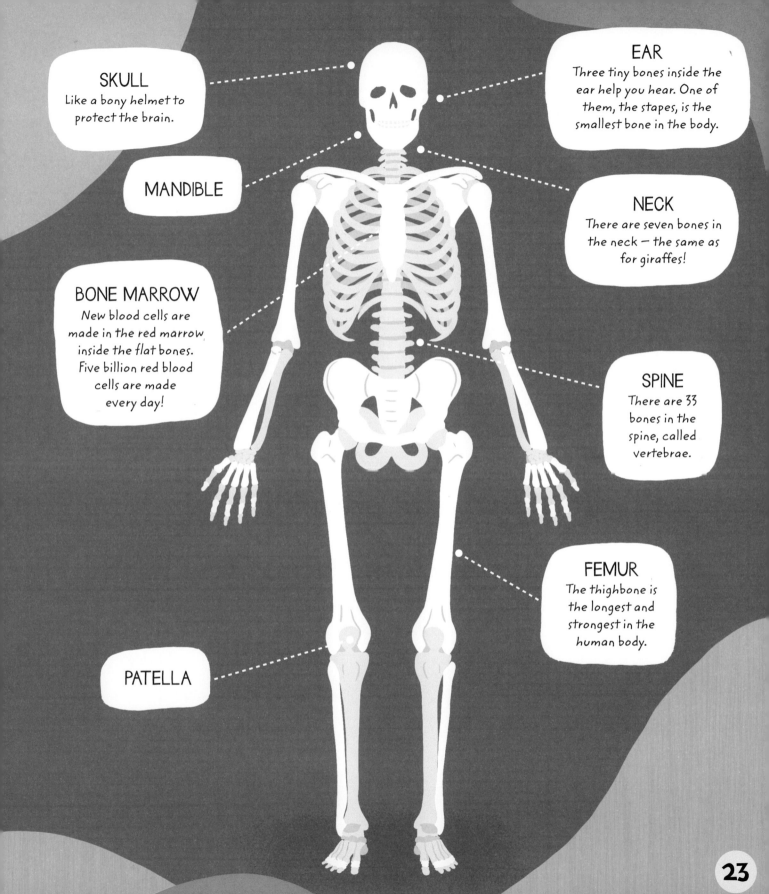

SKULL
Like a bony helmet to protect the brain.

EAR
Three tiny bones inside the ear help you hear. One of them, the stapes, is the smallest bone in the body.

MANDIBLE

NECK
There are seven bones in the neck — the same as for giraffes!

BONE MARROW
New blood cells are made in the red marrow inside the flat bones. Five billion red blood cells are made every day!

SPINE
There are 33 bones in the spine, called vertebrae.

FEMUR
The thighbone is the longest and strongest in the human body.

PATELLA

23

MUSCLES

From big jumps to fingertip movements, and deliberate actions to those we cannot control, muscles allow us to move. There are three different types of muscle that do different jobs. You can make muscles more powerful by doing exercise.

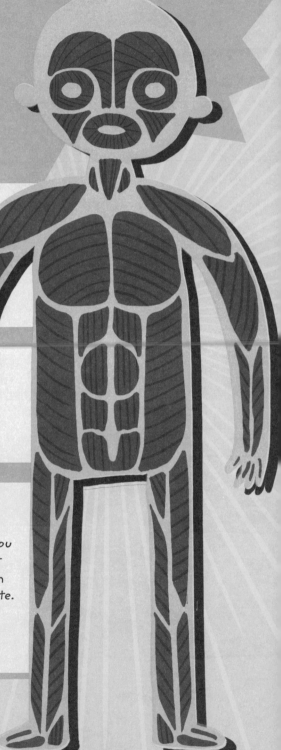

MOVING THE SKELETON

Skeletal muscles are connected to the skeleton by tendons. To move a bone, a muscle on one side of the bone contracts (tightens and gets smaller) and the muscle on the other side expands (relaxes and gets longer). This happens whether you are doing something big like star jumps or very small and precise like writing.

HEARTBEAT

One muscle just keeps on going through your life no matter what! Your heart has been beating since before you were born and will beat throughout your whole life. It is made up of cardiac muscle, which you cannot control.

BEYOND YOUR CONTROL

Smooth muscle surrounds most of the organs inside your body and helps them do their jobs. Smooth muscle cannot be controlled and does what it needs without you thinking about it. Smooth muscle around your stomach helps to churn food about and break it down. Food then passes through the intestines, a long tube covered in two types of smooth muscle, which squeeze food through like a tube of toothpaste.

You can control the muscles that help you to breathe but only for a short while. Luckily, they carry on doing their job even if you are asleep.

Did you know?
The biggest muscle in the body is the gluteus maximus (the bottom)!

Can you find these biology words in this word search?
Words can read backwards, forwards, up, down and diagonally.

```
d t h j d e l q s x y d e o h v p
y o n u p l o r t n o c g i u v e
k t i y t a s k u s e d i n e n a
c g d k c r u s l c o n t r a c t
a a e o a m i t o d a a e i r t u
b n a i r x e o u s t h s i t h t
d l s y d l t t m s v e h l f e a
e a w g i e u o c t d p l m v a i
e t v x a g o e r y d n e u o r l
f e s r c t p e s l n v u s l t p
h l t u h c v i o g a r u c c e o
i e p l y g r p m m p n g l r t f
c k j u r b c k s t x w n e n l e
d s y i s y f d s z e a a i o u r
a y g l u t e u s a m g o c e y c
s e l e e s i c r e x e c s i k j
g e t c u z y s e o j a v t f v a
```

cardiac   **heart**   **contract**

control   **muscle**   **expand**

exercise   **skeletal**

gluteus   **smooth**

Answers on page 32.

CIRCULATION

Blood circulates around the body in vessels. The blood makes a journey that starts at the heart, visits the lungs and travels to every part of the body, bringing what the body needs to work, and taking away the waste that is no longer needed.

The heart is a pump that pushes blood along with every beat. The right half of the heart sends blood to the lungs, where red blood cells pick up oxygen and let go of carbon dioxide. Then the blood, fully stocked with oxygen, travels back to the left side of the heart, where each heartbeat pushes it around the rest of the body. Blood takes oxygen to every organ of the body. Oxygen is what the body uses to do its jobs, from thinking to moving and digesting.

This microscope image shows the different types of blood cell, enlarged many times. Follow the key and colour in each cell the right colour.

When red blood cells are full of oxygen they are bright red. When they have given away all their oxygen and are instead carrying carbon dioxide, they are dark red (shown here as blue).

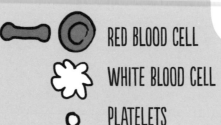

RED BLOOD CELL

WHITE BLOOD CELL

PLATELETS

Count how many there are of each.
Answers on page 32.

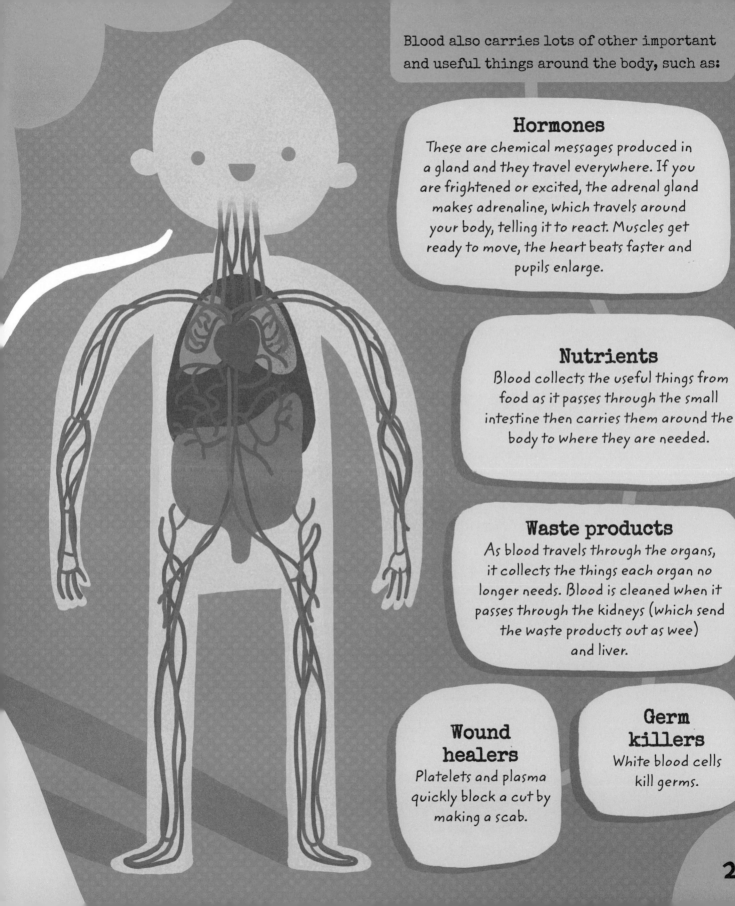

Blood also carries lots of other important and useful things around the body, such as:

Hormones

These are chemical messages produced in a gland and they travel everywhere. If you are frightened or excited, the adrenal gland makes adrenaline, which travels around your body, telling it to react. Muscles get ready to move, the heart beats faster and pupils enlarge.

Nutrients

Blood collects the useful things from food as it passes through the small intestine then carries them around the body to where they are needed.

Waste products

As blood travels through the organs, it collects the things each organ no longer needs. Blood is cleaned when it passes through the kidneys (which send the waste products out as wee) and liver.

Wound healers

Platelets and plasma quickly block a cut by making a scab.

Germ killers

White blood cells kill germs.

FOOD CHAINS

Plants, animals and humans all need each other and each life cycle affects the life cycle of every living thing on planet Earth.

Plants turn energy from the sun into the energy to grow. Animals (including humans) take that energy by eating plants, and then some animals eat other animals. In this way, energy from the sun eventually becomes energy that animals can use. Animals at the 'top' of the food chain are not eaten by anything else. But when they die, they return their nutrients and energy to the food chain when their bodies break down and feed plants.

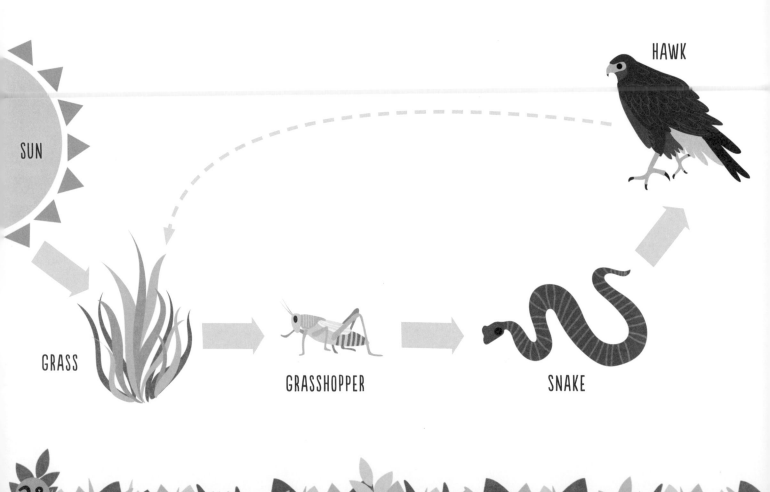

SUN

HAWK

GRASS

GRASSHOPPER

SNAKE

There are many different combinations of plant and animal that make up a food chain but they all start with energy from the sun and end with an animal. Complete these food chains by drawing or writing in examples of plants and animals that feed on each other.

SUN → GRASS → ☐ → ☐ → OWL

SUN → ☐ → ☐ → HUMAN

SUN → SEAWEED → ☐ → ☐ → ☐

ANSWERS

pages 4-5

rainforest

desert

desiduous
forest

page 7

page 9

page 11

page 13

Cold

thick fur keeps them warm

thick fur keeps them warm

lots of fat to keep in heat

Warm

large ears to keep cool

stores water in hump so can go days without drinking

shiny tough skin stops water leaving

page 15

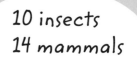

10 insects
14 mammals

page 19

pages 22-23

1. Three
2. Femur
3. Femur
4. Stapes
5. Twelve
6. Mandible
7. Patella

page 25

```
d t h j d e l q s x y d e o h v p
y o n u p l o r t n o c g i u v e
k t i y t a s k u s e d i n e n a
c g d k c r u s l c o n t r a c t
a a e o a m i t o d a a e i r t u
b n a i r x e o u s t h s i t h t
d l s y d l t t m s v e h l f e a
e a w g i e u o c t d p l v o a r
e t v x a g o e r y d n e u a i t
f e s r c t p e s l n v u s l t p
h l t u h c v i o g a r u c c e o
i e p l y g r p m m p n g e r t f
c k j u r b c k s t x w n e n l e
d s y i s y f d s z e a a i o u r
a y g l u t e u s a m g o c e y c
s e l e e s i c r e x e c s i k j
g e t c u z y s e o j a v t f v a
```

page 26

39 red blood cells
23 white blood cells
41 platelets